CW00434020

Acknowledgments.

Firstly, thank you to my beautiful son who so tolerantly puts up with the jokes I constantly recite, laughing when they are (are not!) funny.

Thanks also to 'the wife' for the same reason!

I love you both with all my heart.

To the comedians who wrote many of these jokes!

I can openly confess these are not my jokes – well a few are – and most are from comedians that I've been to see or admire.

I've left some names of the recommended comedians on the final pages.

PLEASE GO AND SEE THEM!

To you....

Thank you also to YOU. By purchasing this book, you're helping spread comedians' jokes. That's what makes people go and see them!

My wife: Why don't you stop telling terrible dad jokes and write a book instead'

Me 'Oh, that's a novel idea'

....

What do you call a ghost's boobies?

Paranormal entitties!

....

Last night I was robbed by 6 dwarfs...

Not Happy!

Farting in a lift.

It's wrong on so many levels!

....

My doctor said that I could die as I have been eating cement.

I'm shitting bricks to be honest!

....

We all know Albert Einstein was a genius...

...but his brother Frank was a monster!

Just seen a burglar kicking his own door in.

He must have been working from home!

....

My wife caught me on the scales in the bathroom sucking in my stomach. 'That's not going to help' she laughed.

Me 'Sure it does, it's the only way I can see the numbers'

....

I've just written a book about falling down the stairs...

It's a step by step guide.

I recently rearranged all the labels on my wife's spice rack.

She hasn't noticed yet, but the thyme is cumin.

....

I had a dream last night I was cutting onions with the Grim Reaper.

I was dicing with death.

....

I rang up the police yesterday and said, 'I want to report a nuisance caller'

He said 'Not you again'

I was speaking to my personal trainer the other day and asked him, 'can you help me to do the splits?'

He said, 'How flexible are you?'

I said 'Well I can't do Mondays'

....

What do you call a magician who has lost his magic?

Ian.

....

What type of magazines do cows read?

Cattlelogs.

My IT manager just asked, 'How does a computer get drunk?'

It takes screen shots!

....

What do you call a dinosaur that uses cheap toilet paper?

Megasoreass.

....

What do you call a belt mate out of £50 notes?

A waist of money.

I don't have a 'dad bod'

I have a 'father figure'

....

I asked my wife to rate my listening skills on a scale of 1-10.
She said, 'You're an 8 on a scale of 10'

I don't know why she wants me to urinate on a skeleton?!

....

I asked my wife why she married me. She said 'Because
you're funny'

I said, 'I thought it was because I was good in bed?'

She said 'See, you're hilarious!'

....

I was going to tell you a joke about a pizza.

But is a little cheesy!

....

Do NOT spell the work part backwards.

It's a trap.

I decided to sell my hoover.

Well, it was just collecting dust!

....

One of my favourite hobbies is to try and pack myself into a small box. I get so excited.

I can hardly contain myself sometimes.

....

I saw an advert in the shop window. '£1 for a TV, volume stuck on high'. I went in and bought it.

Well I couldn't turn that down!

There is a guy that keeps stealing IPhone's.

At some point I am sure he will face time.

....

I really don't trust ladders.

They are always up to something.

....

Black Beauty won the Grand National at odds of 100/1

She was a dark horse!

Velcro. It's a right rip off.

....

Did you hear about the monkeys who shared an Amazon
account?

They were Prime mates.

....

Some arsehole has stolen my selfie stick.

They need to take a long look at themselves!

I have an Irish friend who always bounces off walls when he's had a beer.

He's called 'Rick O'Shea'

....

I was attacked by 1,3,5,7,9 and 11.

I lost the fight as the odds were against me!

....

My wife is furious that the 21-year-old stunning blonde next door keeps sunbathing naked in her garden.

Personally, I'm on the fence!

My bank recently called me to tell me I had an outstanding balance.

I said. 'Thanks, I used to do gymnastics' and hung up.

That was nice of them to say.

....

I asked 100 women which shampoo they preferred.

All them replied 'How the hell did you get in here?'

....

I tripped over in France.

Eiffel over.

How do you make a waterbed bouncier?

You add spring water!

....

My mate keeps saying, 'Cheer up man, it could be worse! You could be stuck underground in hole full of water'

I know he means well.

....

What does a house wear to a party?

Address.

Why do fish always sing off key?

Well, you can tuna fish!

....

I went to the pet shop and asked for 12 bees.

The shop came and give me 13. He said it was a 'freebie'

....

My wife dressed up as a policewoman the other day. She said I was under arrest on suspicion of being great in bed.

After 2 minutes all charges were dropped due to lack of evidence!

Does Sean Connery like herbs?

Yes, but only partially!

....

Did you know that vampires aren't real...?

Well, unless you Count Dracula.

....

The person who invented AutoCorrect should burn in hello.

I just got a job at a cycle factory.

I'm the spokesperson.

....

The only thing I have planned for today is to get my new
glasses.

Then I'll see what happens.

....

I just dreamt of a colour that I had never seen before.

I think it was a pigment of my imagination.

At a job interview last week, I filled my glass of water until it overflowed a little.

'Nervous' said the interviewer?

'No, I like to give 110%'

....

I went to dinner at my new girlfriend parents' house last week and her mum asked how many roast potatoes I would like.

I said 'I will have one please'

She said 'You don't have to be so polite'

So, I said 'Ok, I have 4 then you silly cow'

I asked Arnold Schwarzenegger what his favourite time of year was.

He said 'You've got to love Easter, baby'

....

I went per shop to buy a goldfish last week. The owner asked, 'Do you want an aquarium?'

I said, 'I don't care what star sign it is!'

....

Before my spinal surgery last week, the anesthetist asked me if I wanted to be knocked out with gas or a paddle...

It was an ether/oar situation!

I once had a hen who could count her own eggs.

She was a mathamachicken.

....

My wife said she was leaving me because of my love for tennis and because I am too old.

I said 'I'm only 40 Love!

....

Why was the broom late for the morning meeting?

Its over swept!

What does a gay horse eat?

Hayyyyyyyyyyy!!

....

What do 3 gay horses eat?

Hay, hay, haaaaaaaaayyyyyyyyyyyyyyyyyyyyyyyy!!

....

I am allergic to bread, but I eat it anyway.

I am gluten for punishment.

I love playing football on an airplane. I play on the wing...

....

I was going to tell you a joke about my new hoover....

But it sucked.

....

My new girlfriend asked me to choose between her and my
job as a reporter...

Well, I have some breaking news for her!

Police have arrested the World Tongue-Twister Champion.

They say she will be given a tough sentence!

....

I met a girl out in a night club last week. She said she would show me a good time.

When we got outside, she ran the 100m in 8.6 seconds!

....

'Excuse me waitress, can I ask you about the menu please?'

Waitress: Slaps me across the face!

'The man I please is none of your business!'

My best mate Chuck hasn't contacted me in a while, so I renamed him Huck.

Because long time no C.

....

I was at the Olympics and I saw a guy carrying a long stick.

I said, 'Are you a pole vaulter?'

He said, 'No I am German, but how did you know I am called Walter?'

....

My wife wanted me to bright up the garden.

I planted some new bulbs!

I went into a shop yesterday and said 'I would like to buy a kettle'

The guys said 'Kenwood?'

I said, 'Great, where is he?'

....

The oldest computer can be traced ack to Adam and Eve.

It was an Apple with one Byte.

....

I really didn't think these orthopedic shoes would help...

But I stand corrected.

First time I met my wife I knew she was a keeper.

She was wearing massive gloves!

....

I was struggling to get my wife's attention.

But then I sat down and looked comfortable. That did the trick!

....

Have you ever tried to eat a clock?

It's really time consuming!

My wife gets really angry when I mess with her red wine.

I added lemonade and fruit and she's sangria than ever!

....

My wife says I don't give her enough privacy!

Well, at least that's what she says in her diary!

....

I was walking home from the pub last night and someone
threw a jar of mayonnaise at me.

I thought: 'What the Helman'

A man knocked on my door today and asked for a small donation to the local swimming pool.

I gave him a glass of water.

....

You've got to hand it to short people...

They usually can't reach it anyway!

....

I broke my finger the other day...

On the other hand, I'm ok.

Why do North Koreans draw the straightest lines?

Because they have a supreme ruler.

....

My wife complains when I don't buy her chocolates.

To be fair, I didn't know she sold chocolates!

....

My old neighbour and I are were friends. So much so we decided to share our water supply.

We got along well.

I debated with a 'flat earther' the other day that the world is actually round. He stormed off, but its ok, he'll come round eventually!

....

What did 50 Cent do when he got hungry?

58

....

A man tried to sell me a coffin today.

I said, 'that's the last thing I need'

My mate say's I'm getting fat.

In my defense I've had a lot on my plate recently!

....

Ever wonder what to say when you sister is crying?

'Are you having a crisis?'

....

Where does the dog go when it loses its tail and needs a new one?

The retail store!

My son and I are trying to learn the alphabet, but we can't get past X.

We just don't know why.

....

Sadly, I've lost 20% of my sight.

Sigh,

....

The other day I bought a thesaurus, but when I got home all the pages were blank!

I just can't find the words to describe how angry I am!

I am Buzz Aldrin. Second man to step on the moon.

Neil before me!

....

My sword isn't very heavy!

It's my light saber!

....

I'm giving up drinking for a month.

Sorry, that came out wrong. I am giving up. Drinking for a month.

A man walks into a bar with a slab of asphalt under his arm.

He shouts: 'A beer please ... and one for the road!'

....

What happens when you don't pay your exorcist?

You get repossessed!

....

Dad, are we pyromaniacs?

Yes, we arson!

My friend asked me if I wanted to hear his Batman impression, so I said go on then. He shouted, 'NOT THE KRYPTONITE!'. I said, 'That's Superman'.

'Thanks man' he said, 'I've been practicing a lot!'

....

Did you hear about the cheese factory explosion in France?

All that was left was de Brie.

....

My grandad was crushed by a piano.

His funeral was low key!

Wife: I'm pregnant.

Dad. Hi pregnant, I'm dad.

Wife: No, you're not!

Dad........!

....

My wife left me a note on the fridge says 'This isn't working, I'm leaving'

What a lie. I opened the fridge door and its working fine!

....

A strong blew away 25% of my roof last night!

Oof.

I went to see a physic yesterday. I knocked on her door.

She yelled 'Who is it?'

So, I left.

....

My neighbours listen to really good music...

Whether they like it or not!

....

I just learned the medical name for Viagra...

It was a hard one... but it's Mycoxaflopin

I was really embarrassed when my wife walked in on my when I was playing with my little boy's train set, so in a fit of panic, I threw a bed sheet over it...

I think I've managed to cover my tracks.

....

What do you call an explosive monkey?

A baboom.

....

My wife says I have two faults.

I don't listen and something else...

Is 'buttcheeks' one word?

Or should I spread them apart?

....

My wife left me because I couldn't stop eating pasta.

Now I'm feeling cannelloni.

....

My wife keeps getting angry that I introduce her as my ex-girlfriend.

When I found out my toasted wasn't waterproof...

I was shocked!

....

I just don't understand it.

Chinese!

....

I told my wife to embrace her mistakes...

She won't stop hugging me now!

I just found that 'Argghhhhh' isn't actually a word.

I just can't express how angry I am!

....

I can't find my Gone in 60 Seconds DVD.

It was here a minute ago!

....

I show a documentary on how ships are made...

Riveting.

Where do naught rainbows go?

Prism!

....

I like jokes about eyes.

The cornea, the better!

....

Cop pulled me over and said 'PAPERS'

I yelled 'scissors' and drove off.

What's the difference between ignorance and indifference?

I don't know and I don't care!

....

What do you call a horse with insomnia?

A nightmare.

....

My friend claims that he can print a gun using his 3D printer, but I am not impressed.

I've had a Canon printer for years!

Why would a pig dressed in black never get bullied?

Because Batman has sworn to protect goth ham!

....

I bought my friend an elephant for her room...

She said: 'Thanks.'   I said, 'Don't mention it.'

....

Are people born with photographic memory?

Or does it take time to develop?

What's the difference between a badly dressed man on unicycle and a posh dressed man on a unicycle?

Attire.

....

Will glass coffins be a success?

Remains to be seen!

....

My friend claims that he 'accidentally' glued himself to his autobiography, but I don't believe him!

Well, that's his story and he is sticking to it!

My wife says she wants a divorce because I play to many video games.

What a stupid thing to Fallout 4.

She wasn't playing...

....

My wife just threw away my favourite herb.

She's such a thyme waster!

....

A coworker of mine names Celsius recently retired from work, so they hired a guy called Dave to replace him.

He's the new temp.

I always knock on the fridge door before opening it.

Just in case there is a salad dressing.

....

Steve Jobs would have made a better president than Donald Trump...

But I don't like comparing apples and oranges.

....

The word 'diputseromneve; may look ridiculous...

But backwards it's even more stupid.

Sambuca may not fix your life...

But it's worth a shot!

....

I got hit in the head with a can of coke yesterday.

Luckily it was a soft drink.

....

I'm organising a charity ball next week for people who struggles to reach orgasm.

Just let me know if you can't come.

What did the cannibal choose as his last meal?

Five Guys.

....

I would like to be a millionaire just like my mum.

She always wanted to be one too!

....

How much does a dumpling weigh?

Wonton.

A neutron walked into a bar and asked the bar tender 'how much for a beer?'

Bartender: 'For you, no charge!'

....

Two goldfish in a tank.

One says to the other; 'Do you know how to drive this thing?'

....

I made the mistake of telling my suitcase that we aren't going on holiday this year.

I've since had to put up with a lot of emotional baggage!

Her: At least invite me out to dinner!

Him: I don't go out with married women.

Her: But I am your wife.

Him: No exceptions will be made.

....

I have a pen that can write underwater.

It can write other words too!

....

How to trains hear?

Through the engineers!

I have so many people what LGBTQ stands for...

So far, nobody can give me a straight answer!

....

My teenage son treats me like a god.

He acts like I don't exists until he wants something!

....

A shop owner valiantly fought off an armed robber yesterday
with his labelling gun yesterday...

Police are looking for a man with a price on his head.

Where did Noah keep a record of his bees?

In his Ark hives!

....

A sheep, a drum and a snake fall off a cliff...

Baa-dummm-tss

....

To ride a horse or to not ride a horse?

That is the equestrian.

I am reading a horror book in braille.

Something bad is about to happen... I can feel it.

....

A woman is on trial for beating her husband to death with his guitar collection.

The judge asked, 'First offender?'

She replies, 'No. First a Gibson, then a Fender'

....

What kind of prize do you give someone who hasn't moved a muscle all year?

A trophy.

What do you call and ugly dinosaur?

An eyesaur!

....

My wife asked me to prepare out little boy for his first day at school.

I stole his lunch.

....

What do you call a witch that lives on the desert?

A sand witch.

What colour is the wind?

Blew!

....

What does a lawyer name his daughter?

Sue.

....

My father was a conjoined twin, so his brother was...

My uncle on my father's side.

How many ants does it take to fill an apartment?

Ten ants!

....

I bought a new pair of gloves today...

But they're both lefts, which on one hand is great, but on the other it's just not right!

....

So many people these days can be so judgmental.

I can tell just by looking at them!

The King of Spain has been quarantined on his private jet.

....

That means the reign in Spain stays mainly on the plane.

....

I've been saying 'mucho' to my Spanish friend a lot more often lately.

It means a lot to him!

A naked man arrived at a fancy-dress party with a woman on his back.

Friend 'What have you come as?'

Man 'I am a turtle, this is Michelle'

....

A jumper I bought kept picking up static electricity.

I took it back to the shop and they gave me a new on free of charge.

....

I've just read a book about the history of superglue.

I just couldn't put it down.

My best mate went completely bold a few years ago, but he still carries his comb with him.

He just can't part with it.

....

Has anyone else's gardening skills improved over this quarantine like mine?

I planted myself on the sofa in March and haven't stopped growing since.

....

I just watched a documentary about beaver.

Best damn programme I've ever seen!

My wife and I laugh at how competitive we are!

But I laugh more.

>>>>>>>>>> **END** <<<<<<<<<

Thank you once again! As mentioned at the start, check out some of the comedians that have written some of these jokes.

Darren Walsh, Milton Jones, Mark Simmons, Tony Cowards, Stewart Francis, Tim Vine, Samuel Connell-Dunn, Henny Youngman, Rodney Dangerfield, Stephen Wright, Jimmy Carr, Anthony Jeselnik, Doug Benson, Demetri Martin, Zach Galifianakis, Tommy Cooper, Amy Schumer, Richard Pryor, Lenny Henry, Billy Connolly... and more!

Printed in Great Britain
by Amazon